PAINTINGS AND WATERCOLOURS OF RAOUL DUFY

PHAIDON

RAOUL DUFY

PAINTINGS AND WATERCOLOURS

SELECTED BY RENÉ BEN SUSSAN
WITH AN INTRODUCTION BY
MARCEL BRION

WITH EIGHTY-TWO ILLUSTRATIONS
INCLUDING SIXTEEN PLATES IN COLOUR

PHAIDON PUBLISHERS INC
DISTRIBUTED BY GARDEN CITY BOOKS
NEW YORK

THE DESIGN ON THE BINDING IS
A FREE ADAPTATION OF A DRAWING BY DUFY

THE TRANSLATION OF MARCEL BRION'S INTRODUCTION
IS BY LUCY NORTON

THE PAINTINGS OF RAOUL DUFY ARE REPRODUCED
BY ARRANGEMENT WITH ASSOCIATION POUR LA DIFFUSION
DES ARTS GRAPHIQUES ET PLASTIQUES · PARIS

RAOUL DUFY

IT would be the greatest mistake to attribute to Raoul Dufy ambitions which he did not possess. He was a charming *petit-maître*, in the sense in which that word was used of certain Dutch painters who have since been thought to equal the greatest, and, to a certain extent, in the sixteenth-century use of the word, when it conveyed grace, charm, sophistication, irony, lightness of touch, qualities then thought much inferior to solemn seriousness of purpose. The term *petit-maître* also conveys something of mannerism and preciosity.

Uncertainty about his status often lies in the meaning of the word 'greatness', for it is almost impossible to find a definition of that word which everyone will accept. Historians and critics are often very ready to establish a hierarchy and degrees of greatness, and, so regarded, you may argue about the exact place which Dufy should occupy among the great painters of the twentieth century or, indeed, whether he should be given any place at all. It then becomes apparent how many different *standards of greatness* are used in such classifications.

Dufy is a great painter provided that one does not claim for him a kind of greatness that was not in his nature, capabilities, and purpose. Strength and wisdom, good classical qualities, lie in knowing exactly where one is going and how to go there. There is greatness is accepting one's limitations, and virtue in knowing and fulfilling them to the utmost of one's capacity. Seen from that angle, Dufy's work is a necessary part of the history of painting in our time; for that painting would be incomplete if Dufy did not figure in it, or if he had painted in a different way. All comparisons are fallacious, from the very fact that values not of the same quality cannot be given degrees in any hierarchy of a greatness that must finally rest on quality itself. One should compare Dufy to no one but himself, and the only question to ask is whether, his art being what it was, he achieved the complete fulfilment of his nature and powers of expression. It is beside the point to argue that his importance to the evolution of modern painting does not equal that of La Fresnaye, Braque, Delaunay, or Picasso. If Dufy's work did not exist we should miss the happiness instinct in his pictures, his joyous colour and gay form, his happy relationships between paint and light, people and things. What Dufy painted no other artist could have rendered, because no other possessed his gift for receiving and reflecting sensations of pleasure, light, and joy. There has been no other representative of that essential part of the French tradition since the time of the illuminated Books of Hours, whose miniature pictures are, like so many of Dufy's drawings, both illustrations and formal paintings in their own right. His fine talent as a painter, his masterly use of smooth, brilliant, shining paint, so light and transparent, shows how perfectly his technique suited his artistic feeling. We may thank providence that Naroger's medium was invented at the precise moment when Dufy was precisely the painter to make the fullest and best use of it. By that *means*, for to him every technique was merely a means to an end, he was enabled to carry out his vast decorative composition on Electricity, for the Universal Exposition of 1937.

Raoul Dufy was born in 1877, at Le Havre, in Normandy, that district which Monet and Boudin had already made one of the homes of Impressionism, and which, with the formation of the transitory '*Ecole du Havre*', became one of the most lively centres of contemporary painting. Dufy, however, began with a strictly academic training, first at the *Ecole Municipale des Beaux-Arts du Havre,* where he met Othon Friesz and Georges Braque (a Norman by adoption), then at the *Ecole des Beaux-Arts* of Paris. Of his masters, at Le Havre, Lhuillier had been a pupil of Cabanel, and in Paris he learned under Bonnat. Since originality is one of those talents which must be slowly learned and slowly perfected, he first exhibited careful pictures in the traditional spirit at the *Salon des Artistes Français,* of 1901, but in the following year, when he graduated to the *Salon des Indépendants,* his own independence was firmly established. No trace of academicism remained, no residue of the Impressionist tradition, no symbolism, no literary content appeared in the paintings characteristic of his twenty-fifth year. The *Courtyard of the Louvre* (plate 3) and the *Beach at Sainte-Adresse* of 1902 (plate 2)—a place and subject to which he returned very often—show that he no longer had any inclination to waste time in producing imitations, no matter how fruitful. Dufy, from that moment, was fully himself, in the quality of his observation, in his feeling for life and movement, and in

6

his clear, original conception of colour and colour-harmonies. His sure drawing of form had, thereafter, none of the fluttering uncertainties of the Impressionists, and against that anxious sense of passing time which urged them to arrest the fleeting moment, he set his determination to create a tempo of his own, just as he created his own space, wherein he could move freely within limits that never either worried or confined him. He thus organised his own universe, firmly shut to what was unattainable, but a stable point of departure for that wide investigation of mass and colour, form and expression, which he continued to pursue unwearied and unafraid.

For Raoul Dufy, the 'Fauvist' experiment was as important as for Braque or Derain. One should not think of Fauvism as of a school of painting, for it never developed the character of a collective endeavour, a common field of inquiry. Each painter attaching to it found therein a different opportunity, which, far from crippling his individuality, helped him to perfect all that was most original and personal in his nature. In this respect, Fauvism was very different from Cubism, in which movement the urge to construct in terms of art resulted in the adoption of a kind of common vocabulary. The difference arose because the Cubists were attempting to create a new formal conception, whereas the Fauves were primarily in revolt against the academic and impressionist art-forms then dominant. The Cubists claimed as their master, Cézanne, the creator of semi-abstract volumes. The Fauves, on the other hand, became after their own fashion disciples of Van Gogh, Gauguin, and, more distantly, of Edvard Munch, which explains why they were so closely connected with German Expressionism. There is this difference, however, that whereas the Expressionists, in continuing the dramatic painting of Munch and Van Gogh, rendered a mood of deep tragedy in terms of 'revolutionary' and often anarchistic forms in an atmosphere of intense pathos supercharged with emotion, in Fauvist painting the emotional content, if not entirely lacking, is not the essential quality.

That the Fauvist experiment was a necessity becomes clear when one considers the great number of painters, all very different in temperament and personality, who attempted it. Even Braque's Fauvist Period, short though that was, was of decisive importance in the evolution of his aesthetic. Derain detached himself only

7

when he returned to a kind of classicism. Matisse was the most steadfast adherent and the most determined to develop by means of Fauvism the great colour masses out of which a new classicism began to emerge. The '*manière d'être Fauve*' peculiar to Othon Friesz, Jean Puy, Vlaminck, Mathieu Verdiehan, Van Dongen, Marquet and Camoin, proves how great were its possibilities and how varied the discoveries that could be made by its methods.

Fauvism, as is well known, acquired official recognition and a title at the *Salon d'Automne* of 1905, when it was so named by the art-critic, Louis Vauxcelles. The name made an immediate sensation; for those enemies of modern painting, the critics, who are always at least fifty years behind the times, and prefer no artist to rise above their level, were enchanted to find a label that poured ridicule on their opponents and frightened away ordinary buyers. Fauves ! Wild Beasts ! With such a name how could men of taste find pleasure in their savage daubs? Boronali's stupid joke succeeded in making the general public despise an artistic movement which they already disliked because it was revolutionary. The jeers of those blind and ignorant critics were of the same kind as those which were once aimed at Ingres and are today directed at the abstract painters. They spoke of 'pictorial aberrations', of 'lunatic colour', of the 'indescribable fantasies of men who, if they are not frauds, should be sent back to the wholesome discipline of the schools'—such was the general tone of the criticism, if criticism it could be called.

The very violence of the reaction from the academicians and their adherents justified the Fauves in their endeavours and proved to them that they were on the right path, even though that path might come to a dead end. Even though for most of them the adventure was of short duration, and all the more fruitful for that reason, it had to be followed to the limit of its possibilities. Fauvism, as a matter of fact, was the outcome of studies begun towards the end of the nineteenth century, and thus Dufy cannot be regarded as one of its originators, since he only began to paint as a Fauve in 1905–1906. Nevertheless, his contribution to the movement, all that he received from and gave to it, was of immense importance to him, and without Fauvism he would probably never have become the artist that he was. Yet it became just as necessary for him to leave the movement as it had been for him to join it.

8

When he first left Normandy, his style was naturally affected by Impressionism and profoundly influenced by Japanese prints, whose effect may be seen in the flowing lines, the significant contractions, and the richness without extravagance which is so characteristic of his drawing. In Paris, the pupil of Bonnat carefully studied the main trends of painting during the first years of the twentieth century, and, most especially, the work of Matisse and Marquet. It would seem that final enlightenment came when he saw Matisse's famous picture *Luxe, Calme et Volupté* (1907), about which he wrote, 'Before this picture, I understood all the new reasons for painting. Impressionistic realism lost its charm for me as I gazed at this miracle of imagination translated into design and colour.'

The very words that he used, 'this miracle of imagination', perfectly describe the underlying idea of Fauvism and the prime source of that aesthetic. Fauvism is a victory of the imagination, and there does really seem to have been something miraculous about it, since it was so completely different from the traditional art-forms. Impressionism, itself, which had aroused the same wrath in 1877 as did the *Salon d'Automne* of 1906, had become a traditional and, for certain people in one particular sense, an academic art-form. Thence the need to go further—but where?

'*Imagination translated into design and colour*', Dufy had said. Other Fauvist painters might well have mentioned colour first, because, for them, the revelation of colour was their initial and most vital urge. Dufy, on the other hand, thought first of design; colour came second to him; for, in his view, a revolutionary change in drawing was even more necessary than a revolt in the use of colour. He was less concerned with how to represent objects than with the objects themselves, and, above all, he sought a new vision. 'What I wanted to do,' he said, 'was to carry my investigations further than those of the Impressionists. The Impressionists looked for the inter-relationships of flecks and patches of colour, and that in itself was good. Now, however, we need something more than the satisfaction of vision alone; we need to create the world of things unseen.'

That last sentence might lead one to suppose that Dufy had started along the road that led to the *clairvoyance* of the Surrealists, or that he was prepared to follow Paul Klee in exploring 'possible worlds'. We shall see later that such was not the case, and why

9

that could never have been so. Some miracles of the imagination (miraculous in a sense very different from that of the Fauves) were not for Dufy, whose imagination was always based on reason and who never ventured beyond the threshold of the mysteries. By 'things unseen', he meant simply that aspect of everyday reality which we have lost sight of through too much realism. The discoveries of Fauvism he first used to create greater richness in his mode of expression and technique, and greater possibilities in observation, until finally there emerged for him what might be called imaginative observation, or, better still, the *imagining look*.

Dufy's kind of Fauvism may therefore seem less instinctive than that of Vlaminck and the early Derain, to whom it was almost an essential, less so even than the Fauvism of Matisse, which was more intellectual than instinctive. The systematic use of discordant colour never, or only very temporarily, attracted him to the violent juxtaposition of pure tones, carried to the highest possible degree of intensity. He shared from a distance in that orgy of colour, finding therein the same sensual pleasure that the other artists discovered; for example, the London landscapes which Derain painted in 1905 and the garish colour-orchestrations of the Vlamincks of the same period. Van Gogh had written that colour should be used despotically to give more force to painting. Such despotic colour was the 'new element' for which Gauguin had been searching ('Take the elements of nature and out of them create a new element'), and such statements became part of the aesthetic gospel of the Fauves, stimulating them in the same way that the 'talisman' painted on the lid of a cigar-box had inspired the Nabis. Nevertheless, each of the artists who received that gospel interpreted its pronouncements according to his own lights and gave them different meanings, for the proper function of any oracular saying is to contain double meanings and engender doubts. That is why the new element which Gauguin demanded appeared to some artists to entail the complete rejection of nature, *as it stood,* whereas to others it meant the revival of drawing. Others, again, thought that it pointed to the absolute rule of pure colour, not to mention the demands of flat areas of paint, abolition of shadows, space reduced to the two-dimensional, and broad touches, firmly stated and even exaggerated, showing clearly that the shimmerings of the Impressionists were done with, along with Chevreul and his doctrine, and the divisionism which

10

Seurat had carried almost to infinity. Then, lest such doctrine should in its turn appear too arbitrary, they included a somewhat heavy weight of paint, an emotional feeling of elementary simplicity, and a slightly unsophisticated expression of gaiety, good health and good humour.

Reacting against the academicism of the traditionalists, they felt reluctant to imitate life (Derain had said, 'Where there is temperament there can be no imitation'). It thus became their endeavour to transform life, to represent it subjectively, not to reproduce it. The great lesson of subjectivity came from Munch, Gauguin, and Van Gogh. But parallel with the desire to establish a new art-form based on *temperament* (Vlaminck and the early Derain) there appeared an inclination to return to a classical purity that had been spoiled by the academicians and Impressionists. Who says temperament says sensuality, and sensuality in its pure essence is innocent. 'We must return,' said Matisse, 'to those essential principles on which human language was first formed,' we must have 'the courage to rediscover the purity of the various mediums.'

Treating volumes as flat areas of paint and expressing them by colour, shunning confining outlines and the enclosed form of academicism, searching for greater intensity of feeling, and rendering it in most intense colour washes, meant a return to a kind of original purity, the attaining of that 'state of condensation' of which Matisse spoke—that 'condensation of emotion' which, according to him, made the picture. To the explosive, emotional qualities of Expressionist painting, the pyrotechnics of Fauvism replied by singing the praises of colour, pure in its own right, not used to attempt any approximation to a dramatic feeling which, in that case, was absent.

Dufy discovered Matisse in 1905. In 1906 he worked with Marquet in Normandy. That was the period of the *Old Houses at Honfleur* (plate 7), of *Umbrellas* (plate 10), of *The Decorated Street* (plate 8), and of the *Hoardings at Trouville* (plate 9). Albert Marquet had not been attracted to Fauvism by temperament (he disliked violent colour-effects), but because of the interest which he took in all technical problems. With his keen, subtle, ironic, somewhat Japanese way of observing, he was searching for a synthetic condensation of form, and, until the end of his life, preferred a palette of neutral tones and of delicate harmonies, that scale of greys, so rich for those who understand how to colour it, as Marquet, like the seventeenth-century Dutch painters, so perfectly did. Dufy and Marquet shared a taste for witty, accented, rather intellectual, diagrammatic drawing; they were attracted to one another by possessing the same kind of restraint, the same discretion in experiencing and expressing emotional feeling—one might almost say the same sense of detachment, that distance which some artists like to preserve between themselves and their pictures. They also had in common a sense of humour, which meant that their minds dominated and guided their artistic temperaments. The Fauvist paintings of Normandy do not possess the fiery enthusiasm of the contemporary works by Vlaminck and Derain, in which Fauvism presented its most splendid displays and excesses, but they do show the liberating tendency of that period and the determination to continue in that way of painting, taking full advantage of all the victories of a time full of adventure and discovery.

In the following year, there was a complete change of environment and the beginning of an entirely new trend. For Normandy, Dufy substituted Provence, and now adopted Braque instead of Marquet as his travelling and working companion. It would take too long to discuss here the essential character of Braque's Fauvist period. It was a happy encounter; it produced excellent results; but it was simply one episode in the evolution of that painter. What was Braque seeking in Provence? He was following the teaching and example of Cézanne, and seeing the same landscapes which the Master of Aix had painted. This pilgrimage finally led Braque to l'Estaque, the very spot where the great revolution in the organisation of plastic form had begun. There Dufy stayed, with Braque, reliving the great adventure which Cézanne had experienced there in 1870.

Braque's natural tendency towards Cubism took a decisive turn after this encounter with the stark masses and hard light, the essential austerity of forms and colours, the savage grandeur of that Provençal landscape, which is not so very different from the Spanish countryside. Indeed, l'Estaque became for Braque what Huerto de Ebro is for Picasso. The two Norman painters, however, reacted to it in very different ways. Braque evolved naturally towards Cubism, because that already lay within him; his wishes, his aspirations, his very nature was leading him towards it. For Dufy, on the other hand, who still retained a bias towards the charm of figures and the sparkling effects of reflected light, the experience was less profound, less vital to his development. The strong, stern influence of Provence did not change him as it did Braque, and did not lead him to Cubism, but it did teach him the elements of plastic composition, a fairly new idea to him. He loved movement and brilliance too much to be bound to geometric compositions; he was too fond of that surface tremor which was to him the thrill of life itself. His natural gaiety recoiled from the rather chill austerity that inspired Braque's landscapes in that country and period. Nevertheless, the new sense of plastic composition affected him deeply enough to influence even his paintings of Normandy, when he returned there. It appeared, for example, in *The Regatta* of 1907 (plate 11). In Provence, he learned from the example of Cézanne and from Braque's Cubism a lesson which he never forgot, but at the same time, Provence, Cézanne, and Cubism, remained foreign to his nature, just as he never became absorbed by the German Expressionism, with which he came into contact at Munich in 1909.

Although he felt very remote from artists like Nolde, Heckel, Kirchner, or Kokoschka, he could not avoid being impressed by the tremendous transformation that was taking place in German art at that period, and we may be certain that Dufy's Munich period, which coincided with Friesz's visit to the Bavarian capital, must have been fraught with temptations and enticements. It was not possible for him to join fully in the Expressionist movement. His sensitiveness to surface appearances, his dislike of problems, and that constant sensation of 'inward joy' to which he often referred, would not allow him the heart-rending pathos, the volcanic eruptions in an apocalyptic atmosphere of wild poetic outbursts, like melting lava, in which the various currents of Expressionism fused and bubbled. But to refer to his encounter with the seething cauldron of Expressionism as though it were an ordinary, uneventful visit, would be to suppose that he saw, felt, and understood nothing of what was happening in German painting at that period. Destiny had led him through the most exciting and challenging movements and centres, Fauvism in 1906, Cézanne's Provence, and Expressionist Germany, but he was not absorbed by them. His well-balanced nature and temperament, his sure conviction of the direction which his art should take, prevented him from making radical changes that could not benefit

13

him. His artistic personality was so assured that he did not fear contamination from other influences and, perhaps, he was safeguarded against them by an optimism which to some people is as strong a shield as intense emotion and sobriety is to others.

One can never become what one is not—provided one already is something. Goethe's precept, which means that one should strive to remain oneself in the midst of continual change, presented no difficulty to Dufy, nor did he acquire any merit by practising it. His optimism did not come from laziness or a vacant mind, but rather from fullness of life, a harmonious and contented nature, and happiness in his environment. 'I can give you only a fraction of my inward joy,' he used to say when friends looked at his pictures. His work shows no trace of worry or anxiety, the dramatic content is entirely absent, and each touch of colour, every pencil line, re-echoes like a shout of happiness. Such is Dufy's aesthetic, an aptitude for feeling joy, a will to pleasure, a wondering, admiring gaze, a clear vision of delight perpetually renewed—'eyes are made to obliterate everything that is ugly,' he used to say. The chief qualities of Dufy's own nature and character could not but strengthen and confirm his strong artistic personality, from which his inner harmony removed all trace of austerity.

Although the *Munich Landscape* of 1909 (plate 12) was to a certain extent influenced by German Expressionism, it was simply experimental, and the effect was short-lived, superficial, and wholly formal. Raoul Dufy's particular feeling for nature found its proper home in the climates which both aesthetically and humanly suited him best, the south of France, Provence, Sicily, and Morocco. In those surroundings his delight in life found the landscape best adapted to his aspirations and enjoyment, and he there evolved that serene, unshadowed candour, that delicate grace that belonged to him alone. For him, the words 'quiet relaxation, classical serenity' characterised those sunny places.

At the same time, he never attempted the transitory effects of the Impressionists nor the structural permanence of Poussin. Among earlier painters, it was Claude Lorrain whom he preferred for his broad, gentle vision, his quiet content that required no sacrifices, his subtle balance between the ego and the non-ego. Following Lorrain, he composed landscapes that were neither transposed nor stylised, but were personal creations. He had no wish to reproduce nature or represent it; he invented nature for himself, and portrayed the scene so strongly and ingeniously that a picture by him cannot be confused with the work of any other painter. He loved reality because he loved life, but what he painted was his own kind of truth, firm, subjective, droll, ironical, often totally different from the original reality of the scene. He was deliberately unrealistic, not like the Surrealists, however, who created a world of fantasy, a dream-world. Working with auto-cratic power, he treated the human figure in the airy manner of those who compose pictograms, which is why his figures so often seem ideogrammatic, even hieroglyphic. Then, having freed him-self from representational art, he began to combine pure fantasy, which is intellectual, with the pleasures of contemplation. He refashioned the world in his own image, not the pathetic world of the Expressionists, torn apart by the passions of those who dwell in it, nor the ever-changing, composing and discomposing world of Impressionist painting, nor the scrupulously accurate world of the Naturalists, nor even the essential truth of the world of classical art. His world was not unlike that of the theatre, indeed, we may well ask whether he did not choose the French Riviera because there, nature, the towns, and the inhabitants, look more artificial than anywhere else. Those palm-trees which never manage to look quite natural, those cardboard and stucco 'palaces' of Nice and Monte Carlo, those villages that seem to be peopled entirely by travellers and tourists, might well be stored away with other 'props' once the season is over, along with all the rest of those transitory, glittering, artificial (in the true sense of that word) objects that so delighted Dufy, who, even when he painted 'straight', would only allow reality to appear up to a certain point, for his imagination ruled the play. The *Public Gardens at Hyères*, 1913 (plate 16), the *Nice* of 1927 (plate 29), the *Fishing-boats*, 1929 (plate 38), would make perfect back-cloths for a theatre, without optical illusion or false perspective.

With Dufy, everything was apt to turn towards the theatrical, but a theatre always moderate, discreet, and economical both of gestures and emotion—somewhat similar, perhaps, to the classical French theatre of Marivaux or de Musset, or to a divertimento in the spirit of the *commedia dell'arte*. He never took himself quite seriously, modestly preferring not to allow such greatness and pathos as he possessed to obtrude, in order to stress the excellence of his gaiety, his sophisticated technical ability as a virtuoso.

It is understandable that, having such an extraordinary aptitude for transforming the actual reality into a theatrical truth by
thinking of the world in terms of decorative art, he should have
turned quite naturally to painting decorative designs, first at the
invitation of Paul Poiret, and then of Bianchini, who commissioned
from him several designs for textiles. The tapestry-makers of
Les Gobelins and Aubusson recognised in his manner of treating
space, his unrealistic colour and elliptical form, a successor to
the mediaeval tapestry designers. Indeed, the horizon-line that
runs almost across the top of so many of his pictures is a most
marked characteristic of old French tapestries. It was thus perfectly natural that this quietly humorous, witty theatricality,
this decorative tendency, should be generally regarded as a form
of mannerism, in which the manner of expression was more
important than what was expressed. With Dufy, the manner of
expression was most emphatic because he deliberately allowed
very little of his personal feeling, his worries and problems, to
appear in his work. He liked to affect a rather aristocratic detachment, a sign of refined understanding, mind and heart.

For that same reason, the figures in his pictures are often like
characters in a play, for example, the *Orpheus* (plate 64) or the
Harlequin in the Venetian Manner (plate 65), which he painted in
1939, or the models in his portraits, whose urbane politeness is a
mask of good manners, or again, his nudes—plump, strong,
attractive rather than frankly sensual like those of Boucher. That
theatrical quality provides a sense of space in what would other-
wise be simply a technical study of the human figure. His nudes
are rarely sensual, even in those drawings where he is most
influenced by the fine flowing line of the Japanese prints, even to
imitating their manner of drawing clenched fingers and stretched
muscles. Such drawings lack aroma; they contain no tactile
illusion, and rarely go beyond the purely plastic problem,
which is, indeed, the basis of his portraits, wherein the very politeness of the model's glance forbids one to search beyond the form.

Thus he particularly enjoyed what was theatrical and representational in life, because, at that particular epoch, life was
strange and unrealistic in the highest degree. The social whirl gave
him endless opportunities for diverting himself upon that stage
where all men are actors, playing their parts, partly in earnest,
partly detached—adjectives which may also be applied to Dufy's

16

art. All the places where society met for the delight of seeing and being seen at their most sophisticated pleasures, regattas, race-courses, and drawing-rooms, provided Dufy with an occasion for making amusing observations of astonishing truth. The curve of a gesture, or an attitude, became in a picture by Dufy, as in the *Mangwa* by Hokusai, expressive of the whole character of some individual. His sketches were keen, humorous, ruthless, yet at the same time not unfriendly, for he avoided the malice of the cari-caturists. He liked to strip people of their lies and pretensions and to be amused by their mannerisms and foibles. Never a dupe, he enjoyed the game, and entered into it because he loved it. Yet although races and regattas interested him especially because of the sparkling gaiety of such social occasions, his boats are alive, his sails flap in the wind, and his horses paw the grass of the paddock with nervous hoof in their eagerness to be off.

Dufy was also attracted by the always slightly ridiculous solem-nity of public functions, the strong colours and conventionally stylised costumes at official republican ceremonies. He recorded some of the State funerals of the Third Republic, for instance those of Paul Painlevé and of Marshal Lyautey, with that never-failing delight in story-telling which was part of his love of life and his joy in painting. The face of the period is reflected in his work as in a mirror possessing the gift of irony without insincerity. 'The subject is not the goal,' he said, but nevertheless, social events offered to his painter's eye a feast of forms and colours, especially when some royal and ancient ceremony, such as the *Coronation of King George VI*, 1937 (plate 61), or the unvarying ritual of the *Changing of the Guard at St. James's Palace*, 1937 (plate 60), pro-vided humorous touches to relieve the almost religious solemnity of the occasion.

Future historians will consult the work of Dufy with the same keen interest that is now given to that of Moreau de Jeune and Saint-Aubin. It will be studied for its documentary content, for the lordly freedom with which Dufy treated the events which he portrayed, and also for the irony with which that Norman painter regarded his fellow-men, showing them like puppets, busy, self-important, disguising the essential futility of their bustle beneath a mask of serious occupation. All the events that he recorded are considered with equal interest. Coronations, naval reviews, horse-races, regattas, the circus, and the opera, are all placed side by side in the big picture-album containing the observations of that attentive, humorous witness of the social life and doings of his contemporaries.

Writing of Dufy's role as a chronicler of society, Jacques de Laprade says that he 'portrayed twenty-five years of our amusements' with the same urbane humour and magnificent sense of draughtsmanship that one finds in his book-illustrations. He illustrated Coquetot and de Montfort for the love which he bore the South of France, so picturesque, so cruel, florid, and theatrical. He also illustrated Apollinaire because his own poetic feeling coincided very closely with that of the author of *Le Bestiaire,* and verses by Mallarmé, because of his instinctive sympathy with that writer's genius for expressing and concealing. His work bears the stamp of his age, particularly those twelve years between the *Exposition des Arts Décoratifs* of 1925 and the *Exposition Universelle* of 1937. He set his finger so accurately upon the Paris of that period that one really begins to wonder whether it was Paris that tried to live in Dufy's image, or whether, indeed, Dufy discovered and revealed its true nature.

In an emotional appraisal of the artists of that time and of their works, the major experiences of Delaunay, Braque, Matisse, Picasso, and La Fresnaye, may well make Dufy's painting appear trivial, and, in the frivolous nature of his subjects, it would be easy to overlook the seriousness and importance of his contribution to twentieth-century French art. We do not become immersed in a painting by Dufy, we cannot plumb its depths. That is the virtue and the disadvantage of his gaiety. Because he never attempted tragedy we are inclined not to take his work seriously. His pictures are illuminations of scenes that he happened to witness, and from them he radiates an infectious delight in life, a lively, brittle pleasure. That very quality of giving a sense of well-being, happiness, and freedom from care, should make us realise the important function of his pictures as 'furniture-paintings', in the same sense that Eric Satie, another Norman, spoke of his own music as 'furniture music', meaning that even if we are content to listen inattentively, it influences our spirits and sensations through a mysterious power, which is perhaps that of harmony, proportion and grace.

Dufy's art gives the illusion of facility, but it is very far from being facile, for he carefully removed from it all traces of effort, all signs of study. His flowing line, so like that of the Japanese, followed every flight of his imagination, obeyed every capricious movement of his hand, but the painter was aware of the dangers of excessive facility, and sometimes forced himself to draw left-handed so as to create difficulties and restrain his virtuosity. He needed to control an enthusiasm that might lead him to give too much importance to technical excellence and to his great gifts as a draughtsman. He was an artist in the true French tradition because he laid stress on logic, and on the testing of instinct through the intelligence, also because of his passionate interest in the universe, as is shown by the hundreds of drawing-albums, in which he recorded the multiform truth from life itself.

His line, which he conceived and rendered with a touch most dynamically expressive, is rhythmic, powerful, tense, significant, purposeful. Without needing to learn, he instinctively obeyed the first of the six laws of painting, formulated in the sixth century by the Chinese painter, Hsieh-ho: 'Rhythmic vitality or spiritual rhythm expressed by the movement of life.' Dufy's work contains no hint of such cosmic communion as that suggested by the precept which Hsieh-ho laid down for Chinese landscape-painting. Nevertheless, although he kept his distance from such complicated ideas, he was imaginative by nature and did retain something of the mysteriously primitive character of his serene and fruitful province. *The Peartree in Normandy,* 1928 (plate 36), has the weighty, bushy, fertile appearance of a sacred tree. In the last years of his life he turned towards a more concise conception of form, brushing the detail aside, so as to reveal the essential masses, which he emphasised with strong, rhythmically applied strokes of colour, as in *The Black Cargo-boat at the Blue Jetty* of 1949 (plate 79).

At the same time it is noticeable that the form more and more often escapes from the surrounding contour, as though to avoid anything that might immobilise it in a rigidity contrary to the very nature of life. One of the strongest and most marked characteristics of Dufy's art, an outstanding aspect of his originality whereby he approaches true greatness, is his duplication of form and contour. This is not the result simply of solving a plastic problem, but is the very essence of his philosophy of life, his theory of the universe, although one hesitates to use such weighty words of so light a painter. Dufy's art is in danger of falling a victim to the mistake of those who profess to see him chiefly as a

19

designer and illustrator of great charm. His conception of form goes much deeper than that. It tends towards a range of objects that refuse solitary confinement and more and more incline to blend one with another. When rupture and explosion become necessary to release their inner dynamism, they burst asunder.

Form that overflows its contour was one of the most significant aspects of Cézanne's teaching. Exaggerated and systematised, it became a major argument in favour of Futurist art. Thanks to the duplication of the object, to the separation of form from contour, the object is constantly in motion, because colour and contour are dispersed, although they appear to be about to rejoin. Dufy, who loved the 'Images d'Epinal', must certainly have noticed what happy effects of movement were accidentally obtained in those popular prints from quite small irregularities in registering the colour. He often used such effects himself because they fulfilled his need to vitalise the atmosphere surrounding his objects, indeed, the more naturally static the object, the more effective became the suggestion of movement given by over-running the outline. The eye of the beholder travels from the line of the contour to the situation of the patch of colour and receives a cinematographic impression that might, very loosely, be compared to that of an animated cartoon, an illusion of swift, continuous motion. Dufy used this mode of expression not only for naturally mobile objects such as ships, people, horses and clouds, but also for those which are inert (houses, for example), so that nothing in his pictures might be dead.

He carried such cinematographic effects to extremes in the pictures of musicians at work, which he painted so often after about 1940. The love of music, as such, is at the root of his many recordings of concert-halls, and of orchestras and soloists performing. His sketches for these pictures are well worth studying. In them, he incorporates the rhythm of the music in the body of the player, and does not hesitate to put extra fingers on the hand of a violinist when it helps to intensify the impression of a pizzicato. That multiplication of fingers, used to express the illusory simultaneousness of movement, connects with the evolution of form on multiple planes by that undulatory perspective so much favoured by Futurists, especially Boccioni and Severini.

In this particular way, Dufy's art coincides with that 'state of music' to which Walter Pater thought that painting must come in

order to reach perfection. The beautiful and plastically un-
changing harmony of the sound-box of a violin often appears in
his pictures, *The Pink Violin* of 1948 (plate 80), for example, and
is frequently associated with a score by Bach. Dufy, in spirit,
would seem nearer to Mozart than to the great composer of
Leipzig, but nevertheless, it is the name of Johann Sebastian that
most often comes under his brush. *Homage to Bach* (plate 82) must
have been one of his last works, since it is dated 1952, and Dufy
died on March 23, 1953. The floral wreath that surrounds the
violin placed on the clavichord, before the volume of a score
bearing the composer's name, is music in itself. The calyxes of the
flowers ring out like bells in the joyful upward surge of a fugue,
as the sound travels out into space.

How interesting it would be, had one only sufficient space,
to compare that *Homage to Bach* by Dufy with the *Aria by Bach*
painted by Braque in 1914. In the latter picture, the counterpoint
is far stricter and more rigid. Dufy, on the other hand, saw
broader possibilities in Bach and came nearer to the truth, for
the great composer personified a vast abundance of life, a mixture
of gravity and good-humour, of jollity and religious awe, of
discipline and freedom, all of which must have made him very
dear to Dufy. Braque, by contrast, found in him a sterner justi-
fication of his own requirements.

In his huge composition on Electricity, dated 1937, Raoul
Dufy would seem to have reached the highest possible plane of the
symphonic orchestration of forms and colours. This is true, not
only because into that synthesis of a world enjoying electric light
and music, he introduces an orchestra and a choir to support a
bouquet blossoming with every capital city in the world, but
because that great surface of paint could have had no life or
movement had he not composed rhythmically and harmoniously.
His original programme included the introduction of all the great
men who, from the days of ancient Greece, had sought for a
solution of the problems of energy, and the different manifesta-
tions of that energy, both in nature and industry. Such a subject
might well have produced a vast number of separate designs and
motifs arranged side by side in a pattern. It was Dufy's strength of
character and strong aesthetic that enabled him to succeed
triumphantly and apparently easily, where many other painters
might have given up in despair.

21

From the very fact that he was naturally, biologically, and spontaneously in harmony with life, his brilliant colour and his line, broken by swift, vital touches, were unified in his broad, happy instinct for the truth. The art of this so called 'minor painter' would thus seem to go further than had at first been thought, extending, indeed, to the very boundary which he fixed for himself, and filling the whole of the space contained between those limits. Few contemporary artists appear to be so complete, so *accomplished*. Yet in his pictures, one can never detect the smallest sign of laboured or painful evolution. Dufy clearly has his place in the French tradition of classical painting. His limitations must therefore be understood, not as though they were short-comings, but on the contrary, as proof of perfect understanding, a wise compromise between reason and feeling, imagination and objectivity, in the quiet continuous flowering of his art.

PLATES

PLATES.

SELF-PORTRAIT. 1898

2 THE BEACH AT SAINTE-ADRESSE. 1902

3 THE COURTYARD OF THE LOUVRE. 1902

4 THE ORCHESTRA,
THÉÂTRE DU HAVRE.

1902

6 DECORATED YACHT
AT LE HAVRE. 1904

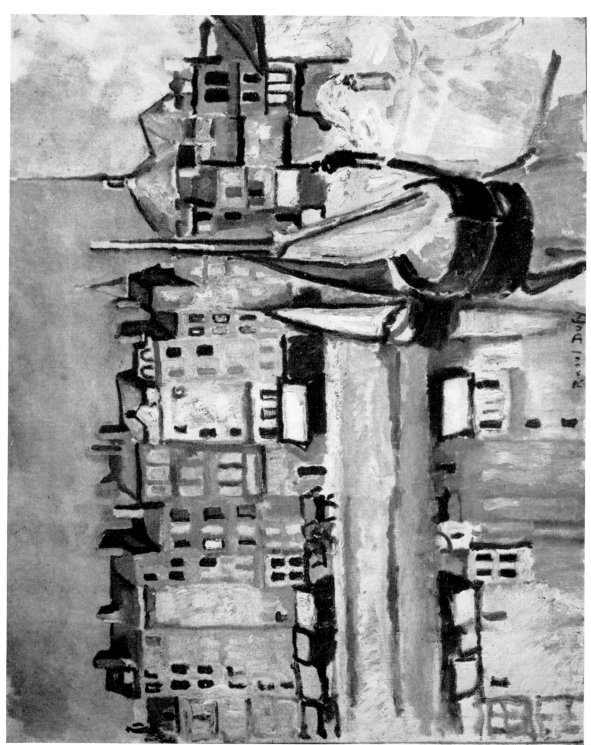

8 DECORATED STREET. 1906

9

10

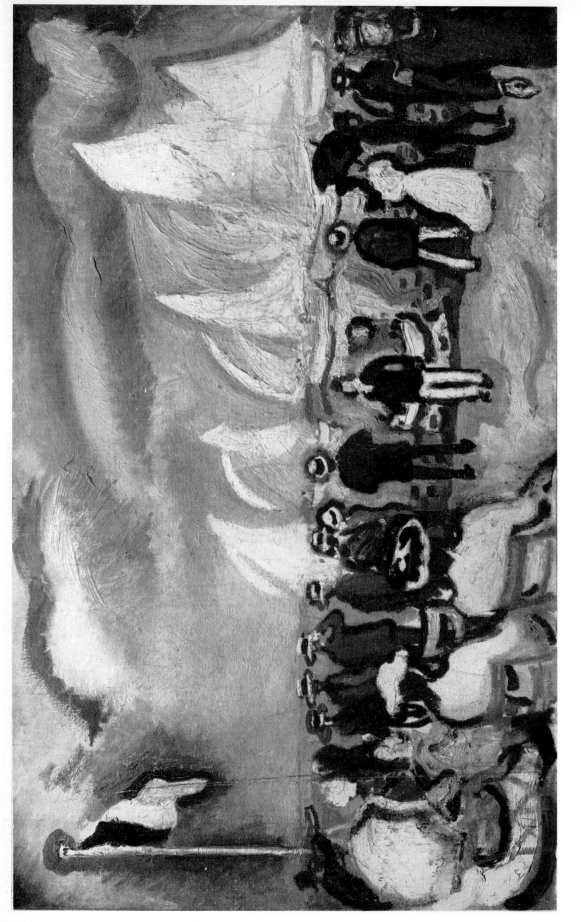

11 THE REGATTA. 1907

Raoul Dufy

12 IN MUNICH. 1909

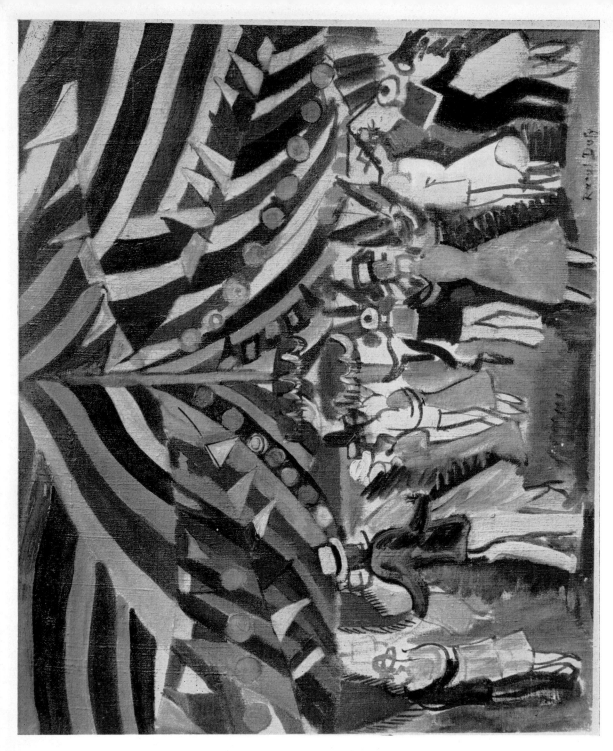

13 BALL AT ANTIBES,
14 JULY. 1910

15 THE PADDOCK. 1913

16 PUBLIC GARDENS
AT HYÈRES. 1913

17 HOMAGE TO MOZART. 1915

18 ROSE IN A ROOM. 1917

19 PORTRAIT OF THE POET JOACHIM GASQUET. 1919

20 BATHING WOMEN. Watercolour, 1920

21 SICILIAN PALACE.
1922

Raoul Dufy

24 SAINT-PAUL
DE VENCE. 1923

25 TAORMINA,
THE SEA. 1923

27 THE SEA. 1925

Raoul Dufy

30 PINE AT
GOLFE-JUAN.
1927

31 MARSEILLES. 1926

32　THE GARDEN OF THE PASHA OF MARRAKESH. Watercolour, 1926

33　THE OBELISK. 1927

34 THE BIRTH OF VENUS.
Watercolour, 1927-30

35 INDIAN MODEL
AT THE STUDIO
IN L'IMPASSE
GUELMA. 1928

36 THE PEAR TREE
IN NORMANDY.
1928

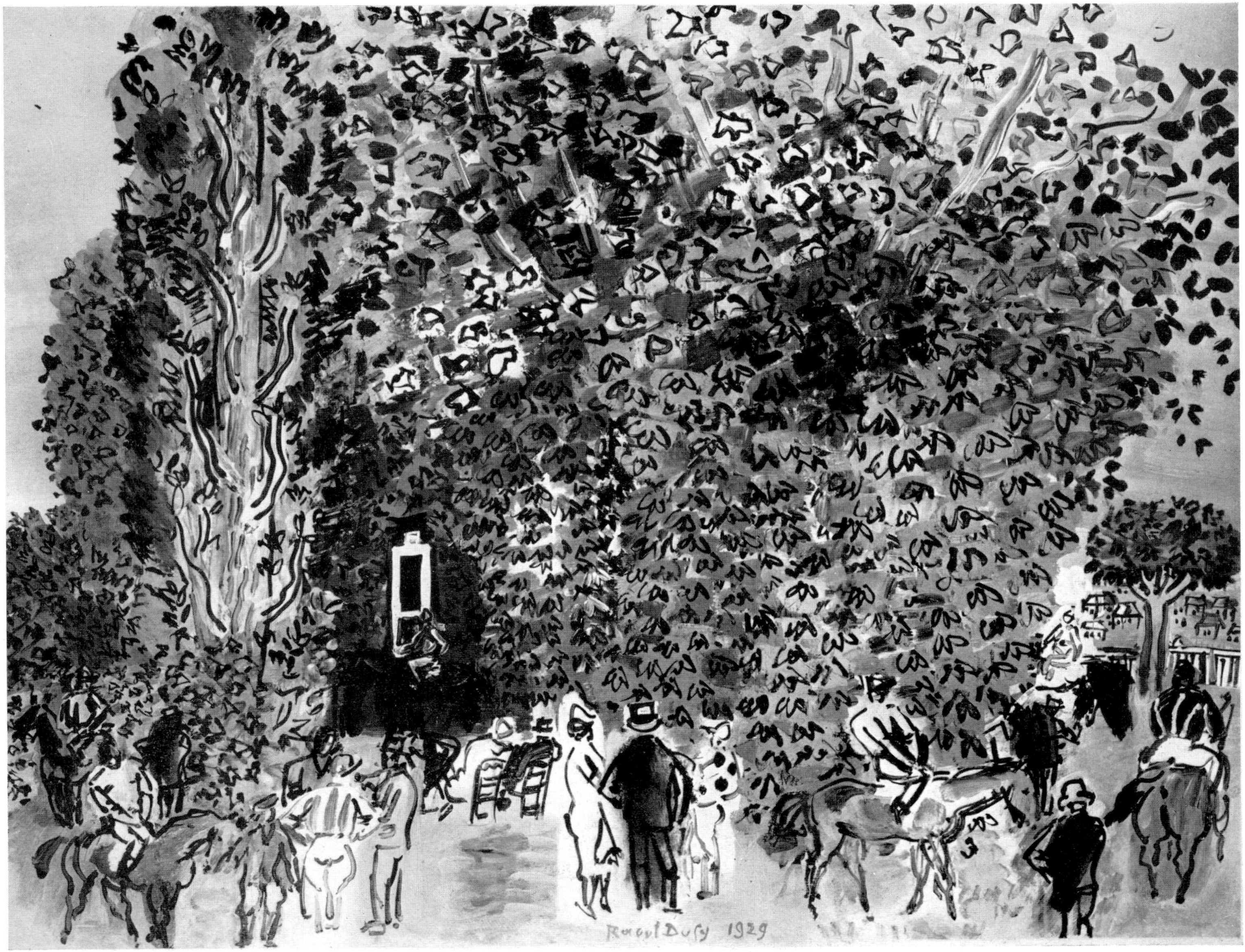

37 THE WEIGHING
BEFORE THE RACE.
1929

38 THE BOATS. 1929

39 HOMAGE TO
CLAUDE LORRAIN.
1929

41 ANMAVITI PONTRY.

1930

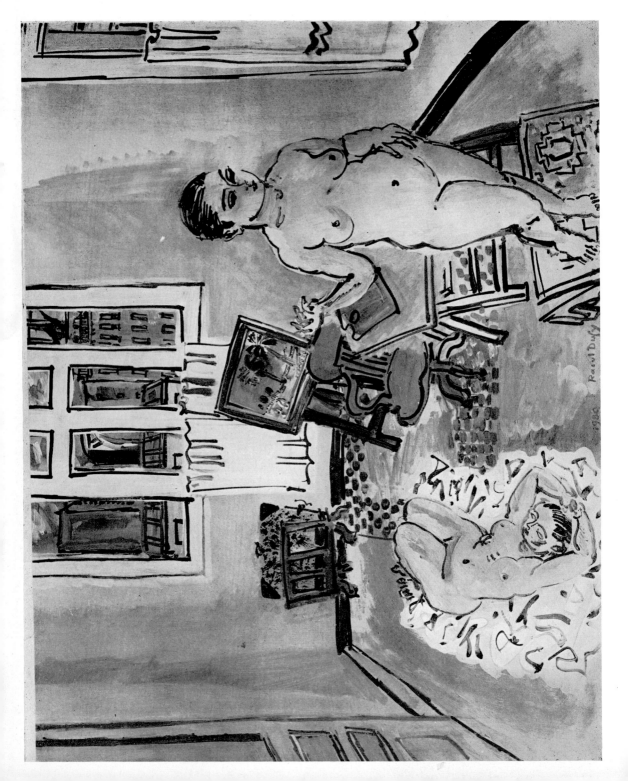

43 RECLINING
NUDE. 1930

44 LONDON,
TOWER BRIDGE.
Watercolour, 1930

45 LONDON,
THE HOUSES OF
PARLIAMENT.
Watercolour, 1930

46 PORTRAIT OF MME RAOUL DUFY. 1930

47   THIRTY YEARS OR 'LA VIE EN ROSE'. 1931

48 THE PADDOCK AT DEAUVILLE. 1930

49　THE HARVEST. 1930

50 ASCOT RACES.
1931

52 JETTY AT DEAUVILLE. 1933

Raoul Dufy

53 HOUSES AT TROUVILLE. 1933

54 PARIS. 1934

55 PORTRAIT OF MICHEL. 1934

56 HENLEY REGATTA. 1934

57 THE CIRCUS. 1934

58 COWES REGATTA. 1934

59 DEAUVILLE REGATTA. 1936

61 THE CORONATION OF KING GEORGE VI. Watercolour, 1937

62 NEW YORK.

Watercolour, 1937

Venise   Raoul Dufy

63 VENICE.
Watercolour, 1938

64 ORPHEUS. 1939

65 HARLEQUIN IN THE VENETIAN MANNER. 1939

66 STUDIO WITH
CORNFIELD. 1942

67 THE STUDIO
WITH THE BLUE
PORTFOLIO. 1942

69 ORCHESTRA.
About 1942

70 GLORIOUS SUNDAY. 1943

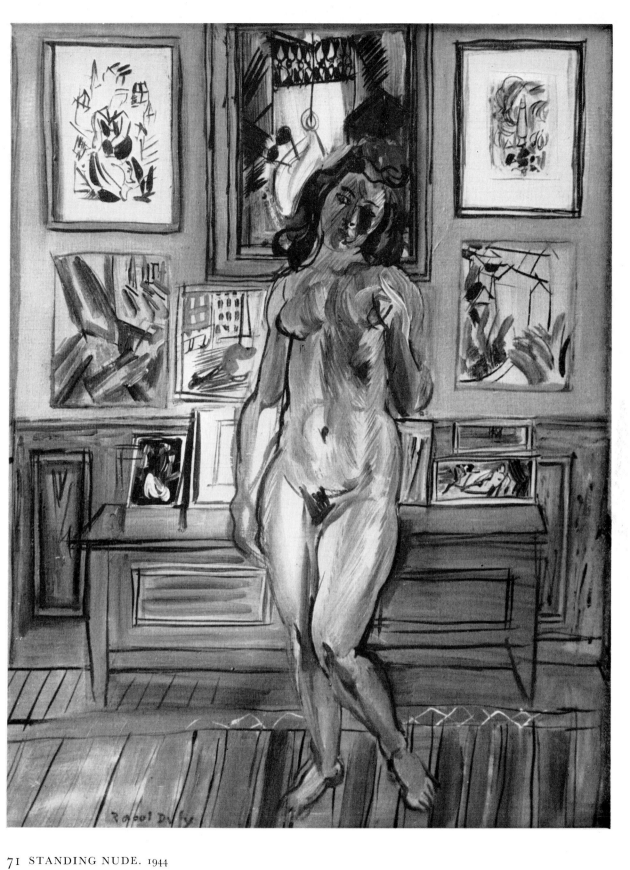

71 STANDING NUDE. 1944

73 THRESHING
MACHINE. 1946

74 INTERVAL. 1945

75 THE DOUBLE-BASS PLAYERS. 1946

76 CONCERT IN ORANGE. 1948

77 GRAND CONCERT. 1948

Raoul Dufy

79 THE BLACK
CARGO BOAT
AT THE BLUE JETTY.
1949

Raoul Dufy

81 MEXICAN
MARIMBA BAND.
1951

82 HOMAGE TO BACH. 1952

LIST OF PLATES

Sources of Photographs

Archives Photographiques, Paris: 5, 7, 48
Arts Council of Great Britain: 64
Bernheim-Jeune, Paris: 20, 21, 29, 31, 32, 38, 39
Galerie Beyeler, Basle: 26, 27, 34
Galerie Bignou, Paris: 2, 24, 30, 37, 41, 42, 44, 45, 52, 54, 62
Galerie Louis Carré, Paris: 1, 4, 11, 13, 56, 63, 66, 68, 72, 74, 75, 76, 77, 78, 81
Cauvin, Paris: 34
Giraudon, Paris: 9, 12, 16, 17, 19, 23, 28, 51
Peter Heman, Basle: 82
Galerie Mouradian-Vallotton, Paris: 36
Marc Vaux, Paris: 8, 10, 15, 33, 40, 46, 49, 58, 70
Vizzavona, Paris: 6, 57, 60, 65, 71, 80

LIST OF PLATES

This list contains the original titles and a few brief comments
on some of the paintings.

1 *Portrait de l'artiste.* 1898. Private Collection, Nice. $16\frac{1}{8} \times 13$ in.
Dufy painted very few portraits, and only three of himself, all of these
in 1898.

2 *La plage de Sainte-Adresse.* 1902. Private Collection, Paris. $18\frac{1}{8} \times 21\frac{5}{8}$ in.
Shows the influence of Boudin and the Impressionists.

3 *La cour du Louvre.* 1902. Private Collection, Paris. $19\frac{3}{4} \times 24$ in.

4 *L'orchestre du Théâtre du Havre.* 1902. Private Collection, Paris. $44\frac{7}{8} \times$
$57\frac{1}{2}$ in.
Dufy's first orchestra, painted under the influence of Degas. Orchestras
were to become his favourite subject in the years 1942–1953 (see plates
68, 69, 76, 77).

5 *La plage de Sainte-Adresse.* 1904. Musée d'art moderne, Paris. $25\frac{5}{8} \times$
$31\frac{7}{8}$ in.

6 *Le yacht pavoisé au Havre.* 1904. Private Collection, Paris. $27 \times 31\frac{3}{4}$ in.
Dufy had a pronounced taste for flags—see his many regatta paintings.

7 *Vieilles maisons sur le bassin de Honfleur.* 1906. Collection of Dr. A.
Roudinesco, Paris. $23\frac{5}{8} \times 28\frac{3}{4}$ in.

8 *La rue pavoisée.* 1906. Private Collection, Paris. $31\frac{7}{8} \times 25\frac{5}{8}$ in.
Dufy painted many versions of this theme, which earlier had inspired
Monet and Van Gogh: gay and colourful streets decorated with flags
on the 14th of July.

9 *Les affiches à Trouville.* 1906. Collection of M. Vinot, Paris. $21\frac{1}{4} \times 28\frac{3}{4}$ in.
A version of this picture is in the Musée d'art moderne in Paris. Dufy's
friend Marquet painted the same subject at the same time. Both
artists, under the influence of Matisse, were then among the "Fauves",
together with Braque, Derain and Vlaminck.

10 *Les ombrelles.* 1906. Collection of Dr. A. Roudinesco, Paris. $23\frac{5}{8} \times 28\frac{3}{4}$ in.

11 *Les régates.* 1907. Private Collection, Paris. 19¾ × 31½ in.
One of the earliest of Dufy's many regatta pictures.

12 *Paysage de Munich.* 1909. Formerly Galerie Percier, Paris. 18⅛ × 21⅝ in.

13 *Le bal à Antibes, le 14 juillet.* 1910. Collection of Dr. A. Roudinesco, Paris.
21¼ × 25⅝ in.

14 *Les régates.* About 1910. Musée du Petit Palais, Paris (Girardin bequest).
21¼ × 25⅝ in.

15 *Le paddock.* 1913. Musée du Petit Palais, Paris (Girardin bequest). 31⅞
× 39⅜ in.

16 *Le jardin public à Hyères.* 1913. Private Collection, Paris. 25⅝ × 31⅞ in.
This picture, painted during Dufy's so-called Cubist period, shows the
same view as plate 33, painted in 1927.

17 *Hommage à Mozart.* 1915. Collection of M. Robert Giron, Brussels.
31⅞ × 25⅝ in.
Coming of a family of musicians and being a musician himself, Dufy
painted many "hommages" to great composers (cf. plate 82).

18 *La rose à l'intérieur.* 1917. Collection of Mme Mathilde Amos, Paris.
45¼ × 35½ in.
This picture shows the decorative bent in Dufy's art. He designed
printed materials for Bianchini-Ferier, mainly from 1912 to 1914, and
after the war occasionally up to about 1930. In this picture the acti-
vities of designer and artist are intermixed. See also plates 47 and 82.

19 *Portrait du poète Joachim Gasquet.* 1919. Collection of Mme Raoul Dufy,
Nice. 39⅜ × 31⅞ in.

20 *Les baigneuses.* 1920. Watercolour and gouache. Formerly Girardin
Collection, Paris. 31½ × 22½ in.
This watercolour is one of many versions—oil paintings, lithographs
and etchings—of the same theme. The earliest, *La Grande Baigneuse*, a
large canvas painted in 1914, shows only the seated bather, with the
landscape of Sainte-Adresse in the background.

21 *Palais en Sicile.* 1922. Collection of Mr. Stephen D. Heineman,
Greenwich, Conn. 23⅝ × 28¾ in.

22 *Canotiers sur la Marne.* 1923. Collection of Dr. A. Roudinesco, Paris. 23⅝ × 28¾ in.

23 *Taormina, l'Etna.* 1923. Private Collection, Nantes. 31⅞ × 39⅜ in.

24 *Saint-Paul de Vence.* 1923. Private Collection, Lausanne. 25⅝ × 31⅞ in.

25 *Taormina, la mer.* 1923. Galerie Mouradian-Vallotton, Paris. 31⅞ × 39⅜ in.

26 *Vue sur Sainte-Adresse.* 1924. Galerie Beyeler, Basle. 21¼ × 25⅝ in.

27 *La mer.* 1925. Galerie Beyeler, Basle. 24 × 28¾ in.

28 *La Marne.* 1925. Collection of M. Georges Daelmans, Brussels. 51⅝ × 63¾ in.
There are two other versions of this important picture, but without the foreground. See also plate 22, of 1923.

29 *Nice.* 1927. Formerly Collection of M. M. Kapferer, Paris. 28¾ × 36¼ in.

30 *Le pin à Golfe-Juan.* 1927. Private Collection, Paris. 32¼ × 39⅜ in.

31 *Marseille.* 1926. Musée des Beaux-Arts, Brussels. 44⅛ × 35 in.

32 *Le jardin du pacha de Marrakech.* 1926. Watercolour. Formerly Galerie Bernheim-Jeune, Paris. 19¼ × 24¾ in.

33 *L'obelisque.* 1927. Private Collection, Solothurn. 21⅝ × 26 in.
See note on plate 16.

34 *La naissance de Vénus.* 1927–30. Galerie Beyeler, Basle. Watercolour, 19¾ × 25⅝ in.

35 *Le modèle hindou dans l'atelier de l'Impasse de Guelma.* 1928. Collection of M. A. D. Mouradian, Paris. 31⅞ × 39⅜ in.

36 *Le poirier de Normandie.* 1928. Formerly Collection of Vladimir Golschmann, Paris. 23⅝ × 28¾ in.
The garden of the country-house of the art-dealer Etienne Bignou, where Dufy spent his summer holidays.

37 *Le pesage.* 1929. Private Collection. 25⅝ × 31⅞ in.

38 *Les barques*. 1929. Formerly Galerie Bernheim-Jeune, Paris. 15 × 18⅛ in.

39 *Hommage à Claude Lorrain*. 1929. Collection of M. Jean Dauberville, Paris. 15 × 18⅛ in.
Fountains were one of Dufy's favourite motifs.

40 *L'artiste et son modèle dans l'atelier du Havre*. 1929. Bernheim-Jeune Collection, Paris. 39⅜ × 47¼ in.

41 *Anmaviti Pontry*. 1930. Royal Museum of Fine Arts, Copenhagen (J. Rump Collection). 31⅞ × 39⅜ in.
An Indian model, who often posed for Dufy; cf. plate 35.

42 *L'atelier aux deux modèles*. 1930. Collection of M. Marcel Mabille, Brussels. 31⅞ × 39⅜ in.
There are many versions of the standing nude.

43 *Nu couché*. 1930. Musée du Petit Palais, Paris (Girardin bequest). 24 × 31⅞ in.
There are very many versions of this reclining nude; cf. plates 34, 40.

44 *Londres, Tower Bridge*. 1930. Formerly Galerie Bignou. Private Collection. Watercolour, 19⅞ × 26 in.

45 *Londres, le Parlement*. 1930. Formerly Galerie Bignou. Private Collection. Watercolour, 19⅞ × 26 in.

46 *Portrait de Mme Raoul Dufy*. 1930. Musée des Beaux-Arts, Nice. 39⅜ × 31⅞ in.

47 *Trente ans, ou la vie en rose*. 1931. Collection of Mme Mathilde Amos, Paris. 38¼ × 51¼ in.
This picture is completely pink, except for the roses, which are dark crimson. On the wall are samples of Dufy's work for Bianchini-Ferier. Cf. plate 82.

48 *Le paddock à Deauville*. 1930. Musée d'art moderne, Paris. 21¼ × 51¼ in.
The first of Dufy's paintings acquired by the Musée du Luxembourg (1932).

49 *La moisson.* 1930. Collection of Mrs. A. F. Kessler, Preston near Uppingham, Rutland. $51\frac{1}{4} \times 63\frac{3}{4}$ in.
The great variety of yellows and in particular the treatment of the wheat stalks are reminiscent of Van Gogh and his drawings of corn fields. Farming was one of Dufy's favourite themes, cf. plates 72 and 73.

50 *Courses à Ascot.* 1931. Collection of Dr. A. Roudinesco, Paris. $21\frac{1}{4} \times 25\frac{5}{8}$ in.

51 *Les cavaliers sous bois.* 1931. Musée d'art moderne, Paris. $82\frac{5}{8} \times 103\frac{1}{8}$ in.
Sketch for a family portrait now in a private collection in London.

52 *La jetée de Deauville.* 1933. Private Collection, Paris. $18\frac{7}{8} \times 43\frac{1}{4}$ in.

53 *Maisons à Trouville.* 1933. Musée du Petit Palais, Paris (Girardin bequest). $19\frac{5}{8} \times 28\frac{3}{4}$ in.

54 *Paris.* 1934. Formerly Paris, Galerie Bignou. $77\frac{1}{4} \times 51\frac{7}{8}$ in.

55 *Portrait de Michel.* 1934. Collection of M. Michel Bignou, Paris. $31\frac{7}{8} \times 25\frac{5}{8}$ in.
The sitter is the son of the art-dealer Etienne Bignou. A copy which Dufy made of this picture is dated 1933.

56 *Les régates à Henley.* 1934. Collection of Dr. A. Roudinesco, Paris. $25\frac{5}{8} \times 31\frac{7}{8}$ in.

57 *Le cirque.* 1934. Collection of Dr. A. Roudinesco, Paris. $25\frac{5}{8} \times 31\frac{7}{8}$ in.

58 *Les régates à Cowes.* 1934. Galerie Louis Carré, Paris. $51\frac{1}{4} \times 63\frac{3}{4}$ in.

59 *Les régates à Deauville.* 1936. Private Collection, Paris. $13 \times 31\frac{7}{8}$ in.

60 *La relève de la garde au palais de St. James, Londres.* 1937. Collection of Dr. A. Roudinesco, Paris. Watercolour, $19\frac{5}{8} \times 25\frac{5}{8}$ in.

61 *Le couronnement du roi George VI.* 1937. Collection of M. Boulard, Créteil. Watercolour and gouache, $17\frac{3}{4} \times 25\frac{5}{8}$ in.

62 *New York.* 1937. Formerly Galerie Bignou, Paris. Watercolour, $19\frac{5}{8} \times 25\frac{5}{8}$ in.

63 *Venise.* 1938. Private Collection, Paris. Watercolour, $19\frac{5}{8} \times 25\frac{5}{8}$ in.

64 *Orphée.* 1939. Collection of Dr. A. Roudinesco, Paris. $25\frac{5}{8} \times 19\frac{5}{8}$ in.

65 *Arlequin à la manière vénitienne.* 1939. Collection of Dr. A. Roudinesco, Paris. $25\frac{5}{8} \times 19\frac{5}{8}$ in.

66 *Atelier au champ de blé.* 1942. Galerie Louis Carré, Paris. $25\frac{5}{8} \times 31\frac{7}{8}$ in. Dufy's studio at Perpignan during the German occupation. Cf. plates 67 and 78.

67 *L'atelier au carton bleu.* 1942. Galerie Louis Carré, Paris. $25\frac{5}{8} \times 31\frac{7}{8}$ in. For the painting on the easel compare plate 80.

68 *L'orchestre doré.* 1942. Galerie Louis Carré, Paris. $31\frac{7}{8} \times 39\frac{3}{8}$ in.

69 *Orchestre.* About 1942. Galerie Paul Petridès, Paris. $25\frac{5}{8} \times 31\frac{7}{8}$ in.

70 *Le beau dimanche.* 1943. Galerie Louis Carré, Paris. $51\frac{1}{4} \times 63\frac{3}{4}$ in.

71 *Nu debout.* 1944. Collection of M. Georges Renand, Paris. $24\frac{3}{4} \times 19\frac{3}{4}$ in.

72 *Dépiquage devant la grange.* 1945. Private Collection, London. $15 \times 18\frac{1}{8}$ in.

73 *Dépiquage à la nymphe.* 1946. Galerie Louis Carré, Paris. $31\frac{7}{8} \times 25\frac{5}{8}$ in.

74 *Entr'acte.* 1945. Mexico City, Private Collection. $17\frac{3}{8} \times 22\frac{7}{8}$ in.

75 *Les contrebassistes.* 1946. Collection of M. Louis Carré, Paris. $28\frac{3}{4} \times 23\frac{5}{8}$ in.

76 *Le concert orange.* 1948. Collection of M. Louis Carré, Paris. $23\frac{5}{8} \times 28\frac{3}{4}$ in.

77 *Le grand concert.* 1948. Private Collection, New York. $31\frac{7}{8} \times 25\frac{5}{8}$ in.

78 *L'atelier du peintre.* 1949. Private Collection, London. $18\frac{1}{8} \times 21\frac{5}{8}$ in. On the easel one of the very many versions of the *Black Cargo Boat*, cf. plate 79.

79 *Le cargo noir à la jetée bleue.* 1949. Galerie Louis Carré, Paris. $13 \times 16\frac{1}{8}$ in.

80 *Le violon rose.* 1948. Private Collection, Paris. $15 \times 20\frac{1}{8}$ in.

81 *Orchestre mexicain marimba.* 1951. Galerie Louis Carré, Paris. $20\frac{1}{8} \times 26$ in.

82 *Hommage à Bach.* 1952. Collection of M. H. L. Mermod, Lausanne. $31\frac{7}{8} \times 39\frac{3}{8}$ in.